MULTIPLICATION

2 x 2 = 4

Ann Becker

Crabtree Publishing Company

www.crabtreebooks.com

Author: Ann Becker
Coordinating editor: Chester Fisher
Series editor: Penny Dowdy
Editor: Reagan Miller
Proofreader: Ellen Rodger
Editorial director: Kathy Middleton
Production coordinator: Margaret Amy Salter
Prepress technician: Margaret Amy Salter
Cover design: Samara Parent
Logo design: Samantha Crabtree
Project manager: Kumar Kunal (Q2AMEDIA)
Art direction: Dibakar Acharjee (Q2AMEDIA)
Design: Shruti Aggarwal (Q2AMEDIA)
Photo research: Poulomi Nag (Q2AMEDIA)

Photographs:
Dreamstime: Gelpi: front cover (center)
Istockphoto: Lisa Thornberg: p. 20 (bottom)
Q2AMedia Art Bank: p. 5, 7, 9, 11, 13, 15, 17, 21
Shutterstock: Anopdesignstock: p. 12, 13; Ingrid Balabanova: p. 5, 7, 9, 13, 15, 17, 21; Buruhtan: p. 20; BW Folsom: p. 14; Paul Campbell: p. 13; Ebtikar: p. 7, 9, 13, 15, 17, 21; Gelpi: p. 1; Michael C. Gray: p. 13; GWImages: p. 5; Kasia: p. 21; Kulish Viktoriia: p. 20; Lana Langlois: p. 19 (bottom left and bottom right); marekuliasz: front cover (background); Robyn Mackenzie: p. 4, 7, 8, 10–11; Pelham James Mitchinson: p. 4, 7, 8, 10–11; Kati Molin: p. 19; Helen Shorey: p. 15; Maksymilian Skolik: p. 19; Ljupco Smokovski: p. 20; Elena Talberg: p. 17; UltraOrto, S.A.: front cover (bottom right); Jiri Vaclavek: p. 9; Viktor1: p. 19; Lisa F. Young: p. 13, 17

Library and Archives Canada Cataloguing in Publication

Becker, Ann, 1965-
    Multiplication / Ann Becker.

(My path to math)
Includes index.
ISBN 978-0-7787-4348-4 (bound).--ISBN 978-0-7787-4366-8 (pbk.)

    1. Multiplication--Juvenile literature. I. Title. II. Series:
My path to math

QA115.B425 2009   j513.2'13   C2009-903374-7

Library of Congress Cataloging-in-Publication Data

Becker, Ann, 1965-
  Multiplication / Ann Becker.
      p. cm. -- (My path to math)
  Includes index.
  ISBN 978-0-7787-4348-4 (reinforced lib. bdg. : alk. paper)
  -- ISBN 978-0-7787-4366-8 (pbk. : alk. paper)
  1. Multiplication--Juvenile literature. I. Title. II. Series.

  QA115.B43 2010
  513.2'13--dc22

                                              2009022426

Crabtree Publishing Company

www.crabtreebooks.com   1-800-387-7650

Published in Canada
Crabtree Publishing
616 Welland Ave.
St. Catharines, ON
L2M 5V6

Published in the United States
Crabtree Publishing
PMB16A
350 Fifth Ave., Suite 3308
New York, NY 10118

Published in the United Kingdom
Crabtree Publishing
Lorna House, Suite 3.03, Lorna Road
Hove, East Sussex, UK
BN3 3EL

Published in Australia
Crabtree Publishing
386 Mt. Alexander Rd.
Ascot Vale (Melbourne)
VIC 3032

Contents

Get Cooking! **4**

Skip Counting **6**

Adding and Multiplying **8**

Arrays **10**

Multiplying by 5 and 10 . . . . **12**

Multiply by 3 . . . . **14**

Multiplication Words **16**

Multiplication Rules **18**

A Piece of Cake! **20**

Glossary **22**

Index **24**

Get Cooking!

Kim and his mom bake together. They will bake treats for a party. Kim's mom uses 2 eggs for a normal cake. But many people are coming to the party. Kim and his mom are baking a big cake. This cake needs 3 times as many eggs.

Kim starts to count eggs.
1, 2
3, 4
5, 6
Kim's mom tells him it is easier to **multiply**. She will show him how.

Kim learns to multiply while he bakes!

Skip Counting

Kim's mom tells Kim that multiplying is adding a number to itself. She asks "Can you **skip count**?"

Kim nods his head.

Kim's mom shows him that multiplication is just like skip counting. "Each group has 2 eggs. So we skip count by 2s. We have 3 groups. So only skip count 3 times."

"Okay, this is 2, 4, 6. We have six eggs." says Kim.

His mom smiles."You just multiplied 3 times 2!"

Fact Box

The word *times* tells us how many times to add a number to itself. It also tells us that we are multiplying!

Kim skip counts by 2.
He counts 6 eggs.

2   4   6

Adding and Multiplying

Kim looks at the carton of eggs. He wonders. He asks his mom if he can find the answer another way. "Yes, you can," his mom says.

They look at the egg carton. She shows Kim the addition problem. They add 2 to itself 6 times.

$$2 + 2 + 2 + 2 + 2 + 2 = 12$$

2+2+2+2+2+2 = 12

Then Kim's mom turns the carton sideways. They add up the number of eggs again. This time they add 6 to itself 2 times.

$$6 + 6 = 12$$

The answer is the same!

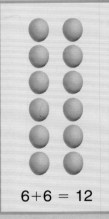

6+6 = 12

Fact Box

Multiplication is adding the same number again and again. This is called repeated addition.

Kim tries multiplication as repeated addition.

Arrays

A carton of eggs looks like an **array**. Each column in an array is a group. Each group has the same amount. We can use the array to write the multiplication problem.

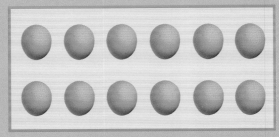

▲ How many groups does Kim see? 6. How many in each group? 2.

Kim writes the addition problem.
2 + 2 + 2 + 2 + 2 + 2 = 12

Kim's mom writes the multiplication problem. She uses a **symbol** called a **multiplication sign**. It looks like this: ×.

$$6 \times 2 = 12$$

total

number of items in each group

number of groups

Activity Box

Look at this array. What multiplication problem does it show?

Kim's mom turns the egg carton sideways.
She has made a new array.

Kim's mom asks Kim to write
the multiplication problem.

2 × 6 = 12

total

number of groups

number of items
in each group

Now Kim knows how to write
a multiplication problem.

Multiplying by 5 and 10

Kim's mom asks Kim to multiply 5×3.
Kim now knows there are different
ways to find the answer.

He can skip count by 3s.
3, 6, 9, 12, 15

He can add.
$3 + 3 + 3 + 3 + 3 = 15$

He can make an array. So $5 \times 3 = 15$.
He says, "Five times three equals 15."

Fact Box

Multiplying a number by 10 is simple.
Add a 0 to the end of it!

His mom says he is right!
Kim's mom asks Kim to multiply 4×10.

He can skip count by 10s.
10, 20, 30, 40

He can add.
$10 + 10 + 10 + 10 = 40$

So $10 \times 4 = 40$. Kim says,
"Ten times four equals 40."

Kim can multiply to find
how many cookies he made!

Multiply by 3

Kim looks at the next batch of cookies.

He tries multiplying by 3. He multiplies 3×4.

He can skip count by 4s.
4, 8, 12

He can add.
$4 + 4 + 4 = 12$

He can make an array.
So $3 \times 4 = 12$. Kim says,
"Three times four equals 12."

Kim's mom turns the tray sideways.
Then she asks, "What is 4×3?"

Kim says, "Four times three equals
12." Then he writes $4 \times 3 = 12$.

Kim made 3 x 4 cookies. How many cookies did he make?

Multiplication Words

Next, Kim's mom teaches Kim the special words to use when he does multiplication problems.

She calls the numbers that Kim multiplies **factors**. She calls the answer the **product**.

Kim's mom writes a multiplication problem on a piece of paper. She asks Kim to label the factors and the product.

$$2 \times 4 = 8$$

factor   factor   product

Kim's mom reminds Kim that times means to multiply. The words "multiplied by" also mean "times".

Activity Box

What multiplication problem does the picture of muffins show? What are the factors? What is the product?

Kim and the party guests think this array of muffins look delicious!

Multiplication Rules

Kim is excited to learn more about multiplication. His mom gives him a list of three simple rules to help him solve other multiplication problems.

Any number multiplied by 1 has a product of that number.

$1 \times 7 = 7$ $4 \times 1 = 4$ $100 \times 1 = 100$

Any number multiplied by 0 has a product of 0.

$0 \times 8 = 0$ $9 \times 0 = 0$ $100 \times 0 = 0$

Numbers can be multiplied in any order. The answer stays the same.

$6 \times 2 = 12$ $2 \times 6 = 12$
$3 \times 7 = 21$ $7 \times 3 = 21$

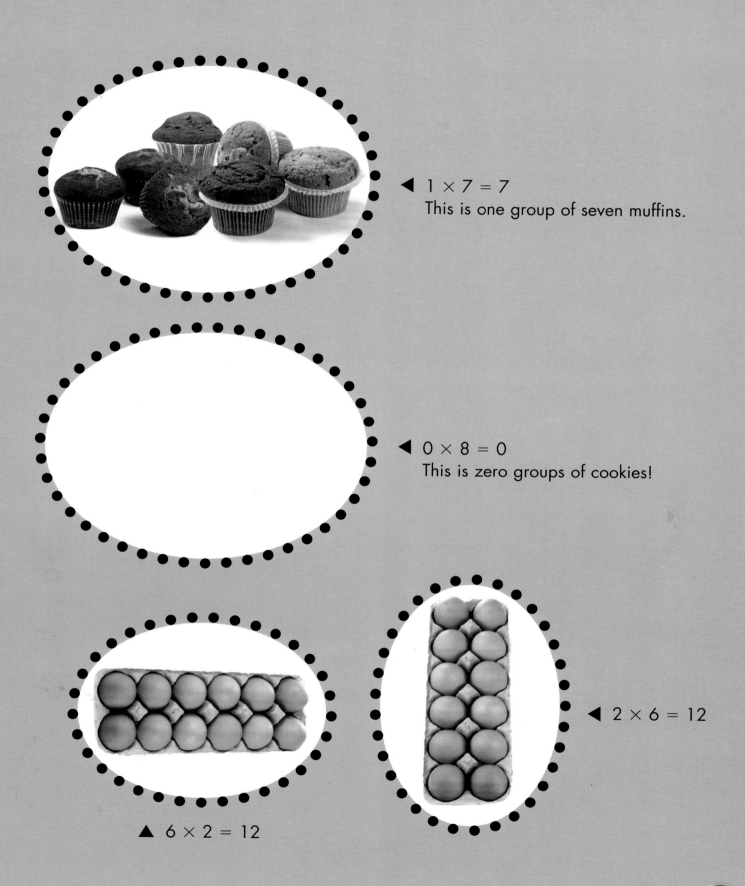

◄ 1 × 7 = 7
This is one group of seven muffins.

◄ 0 × 8 = 0
This is zero groups of cookies!

▲ 6 × 2 = 12

◄ 2 × 6 = 12

A Piece of Cake!

Kim thinks multiplication is easy. So his mom gives him two problems to try. Get a piece of paper and pencil. You can multiply, too!

What is the product of 2 times 7?

What is 3 times 10?

Kim likes baking and multiplying with his mom.

Glossary

array A group of objects in rows and columns

factors Numbers multiplied in a multiplication problem

multiplication sign ×

multiply To find a product of two factors

product The answer to a multiplication problem

skip count To create a pattern by counting by a given number

symbol Something that stands for something else

You can use this multiplication chart to help you learn your multiplication facts.

MULTIPLICATION

x	1	2	3	4	5	6	7	8	9	10
1	1	2	3	4	5	6	7	8	9	10
2	2	4	6	8	10	12	14	16	18	20
3	3	6	9	12	15	18	21	24	27	30
4	4	8	12	16	20	24	28	32	36	40
5	5	10	15	20	25	30	35	40	45	50
6	6	12	18	24	30	36	42	48	54	60
7	7	14	21	28	35	42	49	56	63	70
8	8	16	24	32	40	48	56	64	72	80
9	9	18	27	36	45	54	63	72	81	90
10	10	20	30	40	50	60	70	80	90	100

Look at the column for 4 and the row for 5. They meet at 20. This means 4 x 5 = 20.

Index

add 8, 12, 13, 14

equals 12, 13, 14

groups 6, 10, 11, 19

multiplying by:

   0 18, 19

   1 18, 19

   2 10, 16, 18,
      19, 20

   3 14

   5 12, 13

   10 12, 13

rules 18

skip count 6, 7, 12,
    13, 14

times 4, 6, 8, 12, 13,
    14, 16, 18, 20

Printed in the U.S.A. — BG